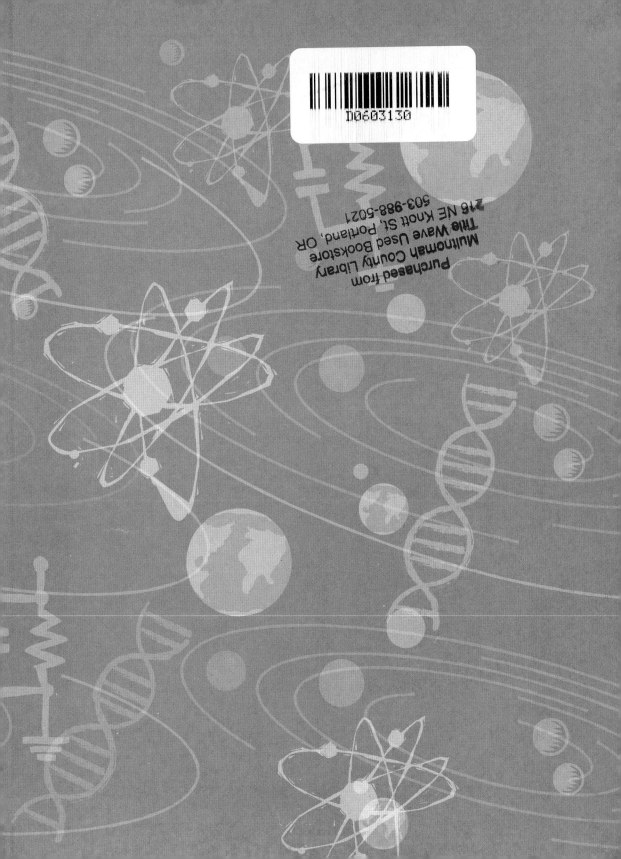

Space Exploration

by Connie Jankowski

Science Contributor
Sally Ride Science
Science Consultants
Nancy McKeown, Planetary Geologist
William B. Rice, Engineering Geologist

MISSION: SCIENCE

Developed with contributions from Sally Ride Science™

Sally Ride
Science

Sally Ride Science™ is an innovative content company dedicated to fueling young people's interests in science.

Our publications and programs provide opportunities for students and teachers to explore the captivating world of science—from astrobiology to zoology.

We bring science to life and show young people that science is creative, collaborative, fascinating, and fun.

To learn more, visit www.SallyRideScience.com

First hardcover edition published in 2009 by
Compass Point Books
151 Good Counsel Drive
P.O. Box 669
Mankato, MN 56002-0669

Editor: Mari Bolte
Designer: Heidi Thompson
Editorial Contributor: Sue Vander Hook

Art Director: LuAnn Ascheman-Adams
Creative Director: Keith Griffin
Editorial Director: Nick Healy
Managing Editor: Catherine Neitge

 This book was manufactured with paper containing at least 10 percent post-consumer waste.

Library of Congress Cataloging-in-Publication Data
Jankowski, Connie.
  Space Exploration / by Connie Jankowski.
    p. cm. — (Mission: Science)
  Includes index.
  ISBN 978-0-7565-3958-0 (library binding)
  1. Astronomy—Juvenile literature. 2. Outer space—Exploration—Juvenile literature. I. Title.
II. Series.
  QB46.J36 2008
  520—dc22   2008007722

Visit Compass Point Books on the Internet at *www.compasspointbooks.com*
or e-mail your request to *custserv@compasspointbooks.com*

Table of Contents

Have you ever stopped to gaze at the stars? Did you imagine what they look like up close? Maybe you wondered if there's life on other planets. Or perhaps you tried to figure out how the universe began.

Since the dawn of history, people have looked to the heavens with curiosity. They have built bigger and better telescopes to see the stars, planets, and galaxies up close. They have presented ideas and theories about our vast universe and then continued to look for more information. Anyone can study outer space, but the experts are called astronomers. They are part of what is thought to be the world's oldest science.

Astronomers once thought Earth was the center of the universe. They believed all the other planets and stars revolved around Earth. Now we know that Earth is just

Telescopes are used to view objects in space.

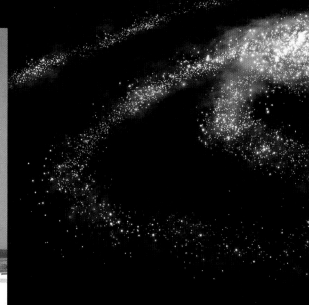

a tiny part of a vast cosmos. It is one of eight planets in a gigantic solar system. And our solar system is a tiny part of something much bigger—our galaxy, the Milky Way. And that's not the end of outer space. Astronomers know that the Milky Way is not the only galaxy. In fact, outer space is made up of billions of galaxies and trillions of stars.

Still Growing

How big is outer space? No one knows for sure. Five hundred years ago, it was thought to be only a little bit bigger than Earth. Scientists now know it is much bigger than anyone could have imagined. Using modern technology, they have learned that the universe is still growing outward in every direction.

The Milky Way is a spiral galaxy.

Patterns in the Sky

Ancient astronomers had a considerable fascination with the sky. They noticed patterns and observed heavenly bodies that seemed to move in a regular manner. They saw the sun rise in the east and set in the west. And as the sky grew dark, they saw tiny points of light appear. Some were stationary, and others appeared to wander across the sky. Most of the lights they saw were stars, but the ones that seemed to wander were planets.

Movements in the sky helped people in the ancient world keep track of time. The position of celestial bodies helped travelers find their way and told farmers when to plant and harvest their crops. People began to write down what they saw, and the study of astronomy was born.

Of course, early astronomers had no idea that space existed much farther than the eye could see. Around 450 B.C., Greek astronomers started using math to study the motion of the planets and to measure the size of Earth, the sun, and the moon.

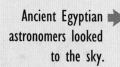

Ancient Egyptian astronomers looked to the sky.

Astrology or Astronomy?

Some ancient cultures believed that the positions of stars and planets were signs of what was going to happen on Earth. They used these positions to predict wars, good fortune, births, and deaths. This system of belief, called astrology, is sometimes confused with astronomy.

But they are very different, and few scientists believe in astrology. Perhaps some ancient astrologers would have made good astronomers, since they were good at tracking the motion and positions of stars and planets.

The 12 signs of the zodiac formed the basis of astrology.

NASA's Wilkinson Microwave Anisotropy Probe measures the leftover radiation from the Big Bang.

The universe is a huge space that holds everything that exists, from the smallest grain of sand to the largest galaxy. Humans have long asked a very important question: "How did the universe begin?"

Scientists who study the universe theorize that the universe began when matter and energy exploded into being. They call the event the Big Bang. The Big Bang theory states that the event happened about 13.7 billion years ago. At that moment, there was nothing but energy, and the universe was too hot for normal matter to exist. Later the universe began to expand and cool, and simple bits of matter began to take form.

A Message From the Past

Did you know that static on your television may be caused by the Big Bang? Scientists say low levels of microwaves found in space are from radiation caused by the Big Bang.

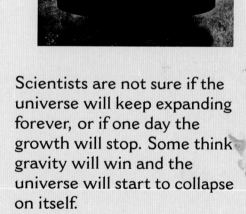

The universe was growing right from the start. Matter eventually spread out to form stars, planets, and everything else in outer space. Even today the universe continues to expand, although it appears to be slowing down. Gravity is also at work, pulling matter together.

Scientists are not sure if the universe will keep expanding forever, or if one day the growth will stop. Some think gravity will win and the universe will start to collapse on itself.

Our entire universe is covered with afterglow light left over from the Big Bang.

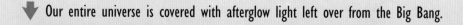

Why Should We Explore Space?

Humans have a natural desire to explore and learn about their surroundings. For thousands of years, people have been captivated by the mystery of outer space.

What we learn from astronomy also affects our lives here on Earth. The U.S. National Aeronautics and Space Administration (NASA) is the largest space exploration group today.

Space travel has helped us in the fields of medicine, computer science, and the environment. Studying how an astronaut's body changes in space has helped treat diseases. And being able to observe our planet from outer space has taught us about pollution and how it harms our environment. In the future, perhaps space study will help us solve even more of our problems.

Information From Space

When you listen to the weather report, do you ever wonder where that information comes from? Satellites sent into space are used to study and track the weather here on Earth. Satellites circle the planet and send back signals and photos. They are able to measure things like wind speed inside clouds, which helps us predict the weather. They allow scientists to track hurricanes and other storms so people have a chance to prepare before a big storm hits. Many lives have been saved by the information provided by weather satellites.

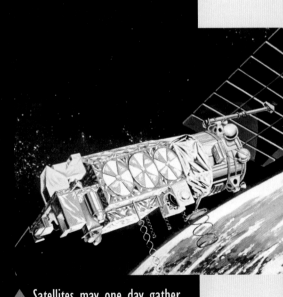

▲ Satellites may one day gather solar power for use on Earth.

Shuttle flights usually last 10 days. The longest flight lasted 17 days, 15 hours, and 53 minutes.

John Glenn was the first American to orbit Earth, in the spacecraft *Friendship 7.*

In 1969, Neil Armstrong became the first person to walk on the moon.

Crime Busters

NASA has been working on technology to give real-life crime fighters the tools they need. Scientists at NASA's Kennedy Space Center in Florida created a device to study a space shuttle after it was in a hailstorm. Lasers helped them figure out the extent of the damage. Detectives can now use this device to study crime scenes.

The space age began in 1957 when the Soviet Union launched *Sputnik 1*. It was the world's first man-made satellite. Four years later, on April 12, 1961, Soviet cosmonaut Yuri Gagarin boarded the spacecraft *Vostok 1* and was launched into space. Gagarin became the first person in space and the first to orbit Earth.

NASA has placed a huge focus on space and space exploration. Its *Apollo 11* mission made the United States the first country to put a person on the moon.

On July 20, 1969, American astronaut Neil Armstrong stepped onto the Moon and said, "One small step for man, one giant leap for mankind."

NASA later developed the space shuttle, a spacecraft that can be used over and over. Since 1981, the space shuttle fleet has had more than 100 successful flights. Two missions have ended in disaster.

Shuttle Disasters

The space shuttle *Challenger* launched on January 28, 1986, with seven crew members. One of them was Christa McAuliffe, a school teacher chosen for the Teacher in Space Project. The goal of the project was to encourage interest in math, science, and space exploration. Just 73 seconds after liftoff, *Challenger* broke apart over the Atlantic Ocean off the coast of Florida. All on board were killed.

On February 1, 2003, the space shuttle *Columbia* was re-entering Earth's atmosphere when it disintegrated in mid-air over Texas. Seven crew members died as a result of the accident.

Did You Know?

Scientists experimented with animals before allowing humans to enter space. The first animal sent into space was a monkey named Albert. Other animals sent into space included mice, cats, dogs, chimpanzees, and even turtles.

Yuri Gagarin's orbit of Earth lasted 118 minutes from launch to landing.

First Woman in Space

The first woman in space was Soviet Valentina Tereshkova. In 1963, her spacecraft, *Vostok 6*, launched and orbited Earth 48 times in 71 hours.

Space agencies like NASA send people and equipment into space for a variety of reasons. Each mission starts with a set of goals. There are two kinds of missions: manned and unmanned.

Manned Missions

Manned missions carry people into space. More than 400 American astronauts have entered space since the U.S. space program began in 1958. Astronauts on board may perform experiments while in space. Most manned flights stay within Earth's orbit.

NASA's Mission Control Center keeps track of manned and unmanned missions.

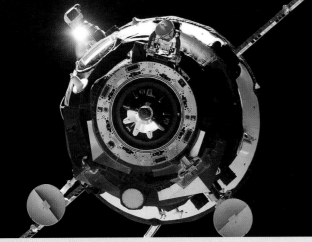

The International Space Station uses unmanned vehicles to bring necessary supplies to astronauts in space.

Unmanned Missions

Why do space agencies launch spacecraft without people on board? Some missions are unmanned when the risks are too great for people. Then people on Earth control the spacecraft by remote control. Unmanned satellites can be used to explore other planets, study the ozone and oceans, or track the weather.

Some satellites orbit Earth for years. Space probes, which travel outside Earth's orbit, may never come back. They explore faraway planets, stars, and atmospheres, sending information back to Earth electronically. Some missions go to places so far away that people could not survive the trip. Space exploration is unlimited, and with unmanned craft, we can learn about places we will never be able to visit.

Meet an Astronaut

Ellen Ochoa is one of many NASA scientists and astronauts. She is currently deputy director of the Johnson Space Center in Houston, Texas. But she started out as an astronaut, becoming the first Hispanic woman in space in 1993. For her journey, she went on a nine-day mission on the shuttle *Discovery*.

Ochoa has participated in four space flights and logged nearly 1,000 hours in space. She is also an inventor with three patents that relate to space exploration.

The International Space Station

Floating in outer space is a huge research laboratory called the International Space Station (ISS). It orbits Earth nearly 16 times a day at a low enough level so the naked eye can see it. In fact, the ISS is one of the brightest objects in the night sky. Sixteen nations have worked together on this space station where astronauts live and carry out experiments.

There have been at least two people on board the ISS since the first crew

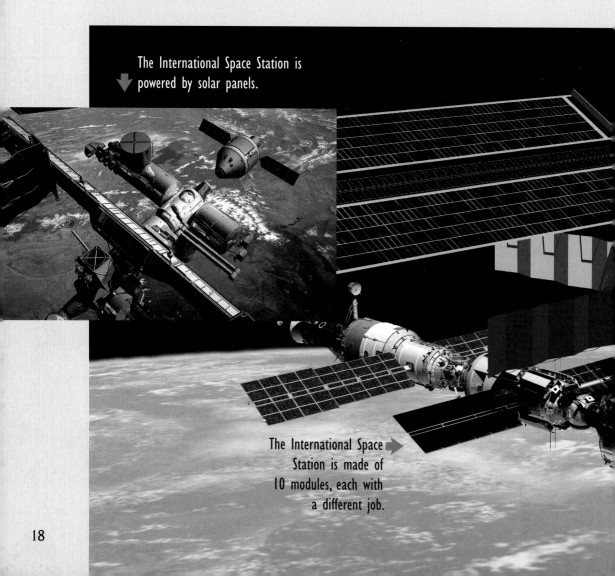

The International Space Station is powered by solar panels.

The International Space Station is made of 10 modules, each with a different job.

arrived in 2000. Most crew members stay about six months, doing experiments and research that can only be done in space. They observe the universe from outside Earth's atmosphere. Scientists on Earth are always in communication with the ISS crew. They monitor their health and help with experiments. One day, the ISS may serve as a launch pad for missions to other planets such as Mars.

A Vacation That's Out of This World

In October 2005, American Gregory Olsen took a vacation he won't soon forget. He paid $20 million for a ride on a Russian space capsule that took him to the International Space Station. He became the third private citizen to travel into space to visit the huge space laboratory.

Space can be a dangerous place. There is no oxygen in space, so humans cannot breathe without assistance. In the shadow of a planet, temperatures drop so low in space that people will freeze without proper protection. On the other hand, if a person in space is in direct sunlight, he or she will fry from the sun's heat.

Spacesuits let astronauts take their environment with them into space. The bulky suits provide them with oxygen and protect them from extreme cold and heat. Their spacesuits also protect them from cosmic rays and other forms of radiation.

Inside the spacecraft, special clothing is not needed once the astronauts reach orbit. The atmosphere in the spacecraft can be controlled. Astronauts put on their spacesuits only if they want to work outside the spacecraft.

Did You Know?

When an astronaut works outside the safe environment of a space shuttle, it is called a spacewalk.

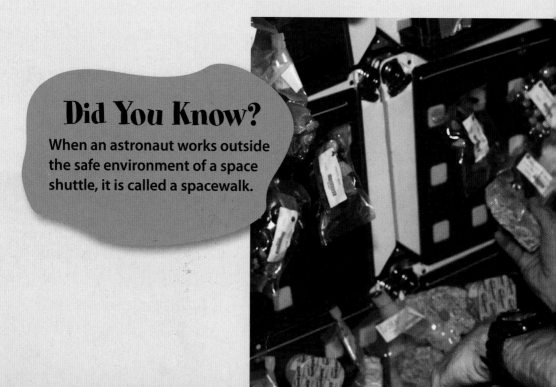

NASA spacesuits are called extravehicular mobility units, or EMUs.

Space Food

Astronauts have a full menu to choose from in their spacecraft. They can eat fruit and crackers or cookies for a snack. They might heat water to boil pasta or cook a meal in their oven. But there are no refrigerators on spacecraft. Their food is freeze-dried instead. Salt and pepper come only in liquid form, since regular sprinkles would float away. There is no gravity inside the spacecraft.

The Great Observatories

An observatory is a place where people can watch what's going on in outer space. Powerful telescopes provide amazing views of celestial bodies. But there are clouds of gas and dust in Earth's atmosphere that can block the view. So NASA launched telescopes into space, giving us a much better look.

These orbiting telescopes are part of NASA's Great Observatories program. The telescopes take pictures of Earth, planets, and stars, and then send them back to people on Earth. Scientists can study outer space without going anywhere.

The Hubble Space Telescope was the first of four telescopes NASA sent into space. Launched in 1990, the Hubble is probably the most well known space telescope. It orbits about 400 miles (640 kilometers) above Earth's surface, controlled from the ground by scientists. Pictures from the Hubble Space Telescope have helped scientists understand many things about space. They have learned about star birth, star death, and much about how the galaxy was formed. Hubble images also help scientists answer questions about how the universe began.

The Hubble Space Telescope allows us to see objects clearly because it is above the clouds in Earth's atmosphere.

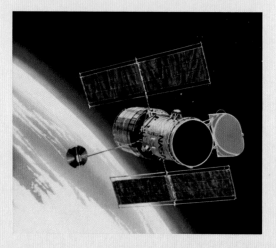

Floating Telescopes

The Compton Gamma Ray Observatory was the second telescope NASA sent into space. It was launched from the space shuttle *Atlantis* in 1991 and weighs 17 tons (15 metric tons). In 2000, the observatory completed its mission and re-entered Earth's atmosphere over the Pacific Ocean.

The third telescope in the Great Observatory program is the Chandra X-Ray Observatory. This telescope observes black holes and other objects that emit X-rays. The mirrors on the Chandra Observatory are the largest and smoothest ever built.

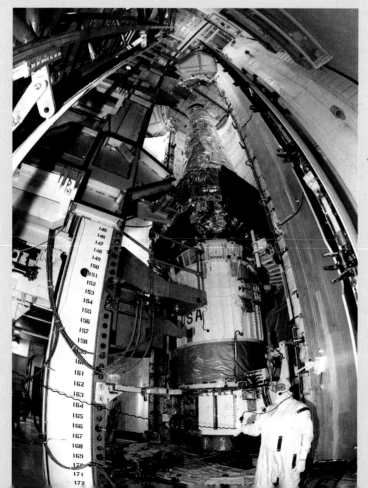

The Chandra X-Ray Observatory was packed into a space shuttle for its trip into outer space.

The Spitzer Space Telescope

In 2003, NASA launched the Spitzer Space Telescope. It is the fourth in NASA's Great Observatories program. The Spitzer Space Telescope uses infrared light to see through clouds of dust in space. This allows astronomers to spot things that other telescopes can't see. The telescope has helped scientists find very young stars and brand new solar systems.

Spitzer is named for Lyman Spitzer Jr., the first scientist to suggest placing telescopes in space in the mid-1940s.

Did You Know?

The Spitzer Space Telescope does not orbit Earth—instead, it trails behind Earth as the planet orbits the Sun. After 60 years, it will have drifted completely around Earth's orbit. Then it will re-enter the atmosphere and burn up before reaching the surface of the planet.

Aglow with Dust

Our galaxy, the Milky Way, is a dusty place. In fact, it is so dusty that we cannot see its center with normal light. The infrared lights on the Spitzer Space Telescope have helped astronomers cut through the clouds of dust and see more than 30 million stars in the inner part of our galaxy.

▲ The Spitzer Space Telescope is the largest infrared telescope ever launched into space.

Stargazing on the Islands

The Hawaiian Islands, as seen from outer space

Hawaii is not only a great place to sightsee. It is also one of the best places to stargaze. Many of the world's best observatories on land are on the islands of Hawaii.

What makes Hawaii such a great place to look at the stars? The dry, still air gives a clear view of the sky. The high altitude and thousands of miles of surrounding ocean also improve visibility.

In places where there are few city lights, the dark sky makes a good backdrop for watching the stars.

The Keck Twin Telescopes were built on top of Mauna Kea, an inactive volcano in Hawaii. Its high elevation makes an ideal spot for an observatory. Each "twin" stands eight stories high and weighs about 300 tons (270 metric tons).

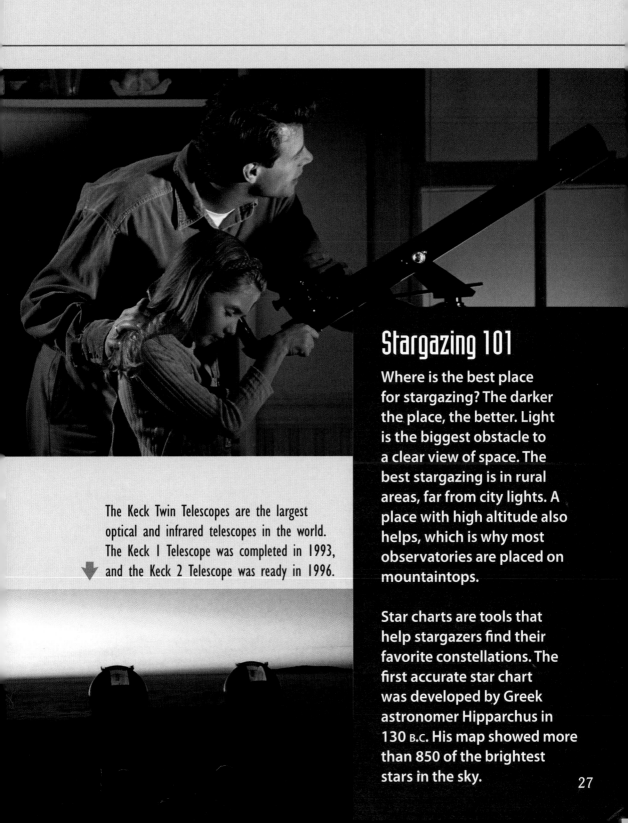

The Keck Twin Telescopes are the largest optical and infrared telescopes in the world. The Keck 1 Telescope was completed in 1993, and the Keck 2 Telescope was ready in 1996.

Stargazing 101

Where is the best place for stargazing? The darker the place, the better. Light is the biggest obstacle to a clear view of space. The best stargazing is in rural areas, far from city lights. A place with high altitude also helps, which is why most observatories are placed on mountaintops.

Star charts are tools that help stargazers find their favorite constellations. The first accurate star chart was developed by Greek astronomer Hipparchus in 130 B.C. His map showed more than 850 of the brightest stars in the sky.

What does the future hold for space exploration? NASA already has plans in place that will take us to new heights in space exploration.

The next manned trip to the moon is planned for 2018. The mission will last about seven days, during which astronauts will produce their own water, food, fuel, and other life necessities. Can homes on the moon be far behind?

There are also plans for a much longer mission—a trip to Mars by 2028. NASA's plan is for astronauts to stay on the surface of Mars for 500 days.

Pluto should also be getting a visit in the future. Pluto is a dwarf planet at the edge of our solar system. In January 2006, NASA's *New Horizons* spacecraft began the very long journey to Pluto. It will reach the dwarf planet in 2015. The unmanned spacecraft will fly past Pluto and send images and data to Earth. *New Horizons* may uncover surprises that will help us learn more about Pluto, our solar system, and our universe.

Farms on Mars?

How can NASA keep a whole crew of busy astronauts healthy and well fed for the two years it will take to travel to Mars and back?

Scientists are figuring out how to grow crops such as potatoes and peanuts in special greenhouses. They hope that the greenouses will eventually be able to thrive under Mars' harsh environment.

◀ NASA's Project Constellation plans to build a base on the moon as a stepping stone for a manned expedition to Mars.

Mini-Constellation Viewer

Constellations are patterns formed by stars. Centuries ago, humans used their imaginations to link the star patterns in a kind of dot-to-dot drawing in their heads. They named the constellations for their shapes, some after ancient gods, and others after objects and animals.

In this activity, you will be making a mini-constellation viewer. When you are finished with the activity, find some of the constellations in the night sky.

Materials

- 35mm film canisters or other similar containers (one for each constellation you want to view)
- scissors
- tape
- pushpin
- constellation patterns (page 31)
- paper
- pen

Procedure

1   Choose a constellation from the patterns on page 31. Trace it and cut it out on the dotted lines. (If you have a copy machine, you can copy it in that way.)

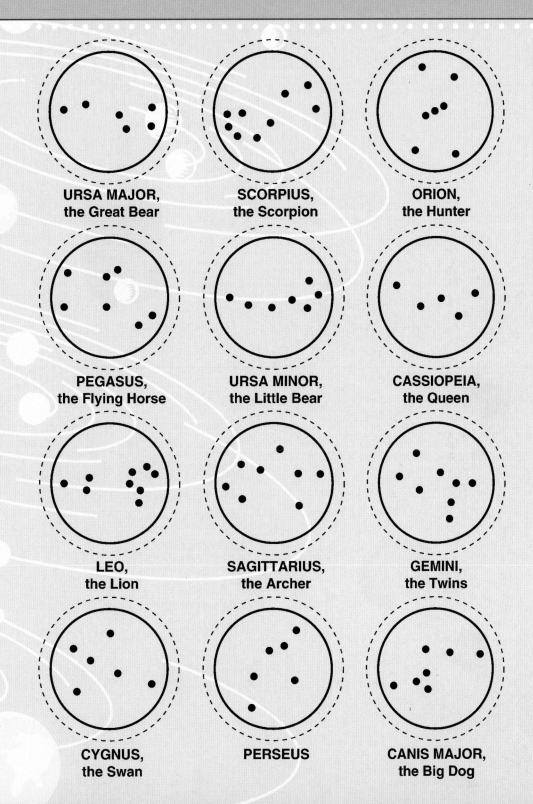

URSA MAJOR,
the Great Bear

SCORPIUS,
the Scorpion

ORION,
the Hunter

PEGASUS,
the Flying Horse

URSA MINOR,
the Little Bear

CASSIOPEIA,
the Queen

LEO,
the Lion

SAGITTARIUS,
the Archer

GEMINI,
the Twins

CYGNUS,
the Swan

PERSEUS

CANIS MAJOR,
the Big Dog

2   Tape the pattern in place over the bottom of the film canister.

3   Using a pushpin, punch a small hole through the paper and the canister for each star in the pattern.

4   Hold the film canister up to the light. You should see light through each hole.

5   Take the pattern off the canister. Trade with a partner and see if you can both figure out which constellation the other chose.

6   Try to find the same constellations in the night sky.

astrology—belief that the position of stars and planets influence human affairs

astronomer—scientist who studies celestial objects

astronomy—study of the universe and objects in space such as the moon, sun, planets, and stars

atmosphere—blanket of gases that surrounds a planet

Big Bang—theory that a sudden event caused the beginning of the universe

Chandra X-Ray Observatory—NASA satellite that observes things in space, such as black holes and neutron stars

Compton Gamma Ray Observatory—NASA satellite that collected data on high-energy physical processes occuring in the universe

cosmic rays—particles that bombard Earth from anywhere beyond its atmosphere

dwarf planet—rounded body in orbit around the sun that is not a moon and is big enough to sweep up the outer objects along its orbit

galaxy—cluster of millions of stars bound together by gravity

Hubble Space Telescope—NASA satellite that observes things in space with ultraviolet, visual, and near-infrared wavelengths

infrared light—invisible light waves just longer than red light waves on the electromagnetic spectrum

matter—particles of which everything in the universe is made

NASA—U.S. National Aeronautics and Space Administration

observatory—buildings designed to study outer space

orbit—path of one body around another

planet—celestial body that orbits a star and is the only object in its orbit

satellite—Earth-orbiting device used for receiving and transmitting signals

solar system—system of planets and other bodies orbiting the sun; other planets around other stars are called planetary systems

Spitzer Space Telescope—NASA satellite that uses infrared radiation to observe small stars and molecules in space

star—huge ball of gas that produces heat and light

universe—all matter and energy, including Earth, galaxies, and contents of space

Margaret Burbidge (1919–   )
Astronomer whose work added to the understanding of the rotations and masses of galaxies; helped design some of the original instruments for the Hubble Space Telescope

Nicolaus Copernicus (1473–1543)
Considered one of the first astronomers, who argued that the planets in our solar system move around the sun

Yuri Gagarin (1934–1968)
Soviet cosmonaut who was the first person to travel in space and the first to orbit Earth in 1961 aboard the *Vostok I*

John Glenn (1921–   )
The third American to fly in space and the first American to orbit Earth; after retiring from NASA, he became a U.S. senator; in 1978, he received the Congressional Space Medal of Honor; in 1998, at the age of 77, Glenn flew on the space shuttle *Discovery*, becoming the oldest person to fly in space

George Ellery Hale (1868–1938)
Founder of three great observatories: Yerkes Observatory in Wisconsin, Mount Wilson Observatory near Los Angeles, and the Hale Solar Laboratory in Pasadena, California; he helped build the first giant reflecting telescope that was installed at Mount Palomar Observatory and named the Hale Telescope in his honor

Johannes Kepler (1571–1630)
German astronomer and mathematician who agreed with Copernicus; studied how fast planets move and the shape of their orbits

Ellen Ochoa (1958–   )
The first Hispanic woman in space on the shuttle *Discovery* in 1993; she has flown on four space flights and is deputy director of the Johnson Space Center in Houston, Texas

Mary Fairfax Somerville (1780–1872)
The first woman to present her own scientific research to the Royal Society of Astronomers in England

Lyman Spitzer Jr. (1914–1997)
First to propose placing telescopes in space; leading expert on interstellar matter, the gas and dust between stars

Valentina Tereshkova (1937–   )
Soviet cosmonaut who in 1963 became the first woman to fly in space aboard the *Vostok 6*

2296 B.C. Chinese record earliest comet sighting

130 B.C. Greek astronomer Hipparchus creates the first accurate star chart

1530 A.D. Nicolaus Copernicus writes *On the Revolutions of the Heavenly Spheres*

1577 Tycho Brahe views a comet, inspiring him to draw a cosmic model of the sky with Earth as the center of the universe

1605 Johannes Kepler formulates his Three Laws of Planetary Motion

1608 Dutchman Hans Lippershey applies for a patent for the first telescope

1610 Galileo Galilei uses a telescope to observe heavenly bodies and discovers four largest satellites of Jupiter

1786 Caroline Herschel is the first woman to discover a comet

1839 The Harvard College Observatory, the first official observatory in the United States, is built

1895 George Ellery Hale founds *The Astrophysical Journal*

1925 Annie Jump Cannon receives the first and only honorary doctorate given to a woman by Oxford University in England

1929	Edwin Hubble formulates Hubble's Law, which helps astronomers determine the age and growth of the universe
1948	The Hale Telescope is opened on Mount Palomar, California
1957	Soviet Union launches *Sputnik 1*, the world's first artificial satellite, into space, beginning the Space Age
1958	Eager to join the Space Age, the United States forms the National Aeronautics and Space Administration (NASA)
1969	Americans Neil Armstrong and Buzz Aldrin are the first humans to land on the moon
1972	Margaret Burbidge declines the Annie J. Cannon award because it is only awarded to women
1983	Sally Ride becomes the first American woman and the youngest American astronaut to enter outer space
1990	The Hubble Space Telescope is launched into space, 44 years after Lyman Spitzer Jr. first proposed the idea
2006	Astronomers decide there are only eight planets in our solar system and reclassify Pluto as a dwarf planet
2008	A powerful gamma ray burst becomes the most distant object ever seen with the naked eye; the explosion occured 7.5 billion years ago

Briggs, Carole S. *Women Space Pioneers*. Minneapolis: Lerner Publications Co., 2005.

Harland, David. *Space Exploration 2008*. New York: Springer, 2007.

Nardo, Don. *Tycho Brahe: Pioneer of Astronomy*. Minneapolis: Compass Point Books, 2008.

Rau, Dana Meachen. *The International Space Station*. Minneapolis: Compass Point Books, 2005.

Voelkel, James R. *Johannes Kepler and the New Astronomy*. New York: Oxford University Press, 1999.

Zannos, Susan. *Edwin Hubble and the Theory of the Expanding Universe*. Hockessin, Del.: Mitchell Lane Publishers, 2004.

On the Web

For more information on this topic, use FactHound.

1. Go to *www.facthound.com*

2. Type in this book ID: 0756539587

3. Click on the *Fetch It* button.

FactHound will find the best Web sites for you.

Index

Connie Jankowski

Connie Jankowski is a seasoned journalist, marketing expert, public relations consultant, and teacher. Her education includes a bachelor of arts from the University of Pittsburgh and graduate study at Pitt. She has worked in publishing, public relations, and marketing for the past 25 years. She is the author of 11 books and hundreds of magazine articles.

Image Credits